DEVELOPING SPIRITUAL MUSCLES

The wise prevail through great power, and those who have knowledge muster their strength.
Proverbs 24:5

by
Franklin N. Abazie

Developing Spiritual Muscles
COPYRIGHT 2016 BY Franklin N Abazie
ISBN: 978-1-945133-12-1

All right reserved. This book or any portion thereof may not be reproduced or used in any manner whatsoever without the express written permission of the publisher, except for the use of brief quotations in a book review. All Bible quotes are from King James Version and others as noted.

Published by: F N ABAZIE PUBLISHING HOUSE—aka, Empowerment Bookstore

That I may publish with the voice of thanksgiving and tell of all thy wondrous works.
Psalms 26:7

To order additional copies, wholesales or booking call:
the Church office (973-372-7518)
or Empowerment Bookstore Hotline (973-393-8518)

Worship address:
343 Sanford Avenue, Newark, New Jersey 07106
Administrative Head Office address:
33 Schley Street Newark New Jersey 07112
Email: pastorfranknto@yahoo.com
Website www.fnabaziehealingministries.org
Publishing House: www.fnabaziepublishinghouse.org

This book is a production of F N Abazie Publishing House. A publication Arms of Miracle of God Ministries 2016.
First Edition

CONTENTS

THE MANDATE OF THE COMMISSION....................iv
ARMS OF THE COMMISSION...................…........v
INTRODUCTION..vi
CHAPTER 1
The Lifestyle of Fasting & Prayer.............................1
CHAPTER 2
Intense Study of the Word of God..........................17
CHAPTER 3
Understanding Mentorship...................................38
CHAPTER 4
Prayer of Salvation..54
CHAPTER 5
About the Author..63

THE MANDATE OF THE COMMISSION

"The moment is due to impact your world through the revival of the healing & miracle ministry of Jesus Christ of Nazareth.

"I am sending you to restore health unto thee and I will heal thee of thy wounds, said the Lord of Host."

ARMS OF THE COMMISSION

1) F N Abazie Ministries—Miracle of God Ministries (Miracle Chapel Intl)

2) F N Abazie TV Ministries: Global Television Ministry Outreach

3) F N Abazie Radio Ministries: Radio Broadcasting Outreach

4) F N Abazie Publishing House: Book Publication

5) F N Abazie Bible School: also called Word of Healing Bible School (W.O.H.B.S.)

6) F N Abazie Evangelistic Ass: Miracle of God Ministries: Global Crusade

7) Empowerment Bookstore: Book distribution

8) F N Abazie Helping Hands: Meeting the Help of the Needy Worldwide

9) F N Abazie Disaster Recovery Mission: Global Disaster Recovery

10) F N Abazie Prison Ministry: Prison Ministry For All Convicts "Second Chance"

Some of our ministry arms are awaiting the appointed time to commence.

INTRODUCTION

"Jesus calls us to his rest, and meekness is His method. The meek man cares not at all who is greater than he, for he has long ago decided that the esteem of the world is not worth the effort."
~A.W. Tazer, Pursuit of God

Without contradiction, everyone interested in developing spiritual muscles must first and foremost develop the spirit of meekness as a lifestyle. It is my joy to bring this publication to light because of a few troubling reasons. My sole reason for writing this book can be summarized in one sentence: ***"The church of God is under attack by the adversaries."***

In my few years of coming to light with the Lord Jesus, I have witnessed a few sudden happening to men/women of God even in their very place of worship. Some of our acclaimed men/women of God are not sensitive to the voice of the Holy Spirit. In my own understanding some of us are preaching just what we want our congregation to hear, we have turned into motivational speakers that is why the devil is causing sudden destruction to the house of God.

This publication will help anyone seeking for the truth about Gods power to return back to the old proven bible approved methods to develop strength. We, as believers no longer fast and pray anymore that is why pastors are slumping to death in their church offices. If we must develop our spiritual muscles we must follow all the approved ways generated by the Holy bible. It is my delight to speak the mind of God concerning *Developing Spiritual Muscles*. Developing spiritual muscles is not cheap talk. *"For the kingdom of God is not in word, but in power."* (1 Corinthians 4:20)

> *Howbeit this kind goeth not out but by prayer and fasting.*
> **Matthew 17:21**

This publication is projected to enforce the laws of the spirit and to help all spiritual men/women engage and wage proper warfare against the wiles of the devil. It is written, *"For I am not ashamed of the gospel of Christ: for it is the power of God unto salvation to everyone that believeth; to the Jew first, and also to the Greek."* (Romans 1:16)

Although there are certain spirit that will not surrender and give up their assaults and attacks, every one eager to develop spiritual muscles must consciously pray and fast as often, orderly and discipline themselves with fasting, and diligently and intensely study and comprehend the Holy Bible.

Remember...

"Then certain of the vagabond Jews, exorcists, took upon them to call over them which had evil spirits the name of the Lord Jesus, saying, We adjure you by Jesus whom Paul preacheth. And there were seven sons of one Sceva, a Jew, and

chief of the priests, which did so. And the evil spirit answered and said, Jesus I know, and Paul I know; but who are ye? And the man in whom the evil spirit was leaped on them, and overcame them, and prevailed against them, so that they fled out of that house naked and wounded." (Acts 19:13-16)

May you encounter revelation and power to withstand the devil and to confront all prevailing challenges in your life as you read this book. May the pages of this book bring fresh revelation to your spirit.

Happy reading.

HOW DO WE DEVELOP SPIRITUAL MUSCLES?

WE MUST DEVELOP A MEEK & HUMBLE SPIRIT

Likewise, ye younger, submit yourselves unto the elder. Yea, all of you be subject one to another, and be clothed with humility: for God resisteth the proud, and giveth grace to the humble. Humble yourselves therefore under the mighty hand of God, that he may exalt you in due time.
1 Peter 5:5-6

Before we train to fast and pray and to study the Holy bible we must covet a meek and a humble spirit. God despises the proud and the arrogant. Anyone who is not willing to humble themselves in the things of God as a lifestyle is not ready to develop spiritual muscles. *"He hath put down the mighty from their seats, and exalted them of low degree."* (Luke 1:52)

Among the qualities that made Moses the greatest of the prophets that ever lived was a meek spirit. *"Now the man Moses was very meek, above all the men which were upon the face of the earth."* (Numbers 12:3)

> *And there arose not a prophet since in Israel like unto Moses, whom the Lord knew face to face.*
> **Deuteronomy 34:10**

Remember...

> *But he giveth more grace. Wherefore he saith, God resisteth the proud, but giveth grace unto the humble.*
> **James 4:6**

We must all desire meekness as a lifestyle if we must develop spiritual muscles in our life time. *"It is written Blessed are the meek: for they shall inherit the earth."* (Matthew 5:5)

Meekness is the quality that exalted Jesus above every other name. *"And being found in fashion as a man, he humbled himself, and became obedient unto death, even the death of the cross. Wherefore God also hath highly exalted him, and given him a name which is above every name."* (Philipians 2:8-9)

Every time we exhibit meekness and a willingness to learn with a humble spirit, everyone around us with relevant information will want to help us succeed in life. I admonish you—humble yourself and embrace meekness as a virtue and watch God decorate your life with unquestionable breakthroughs and promotions.

WE MUST BE WILLING TO LEARN

It is proven that proud people do not secure help from any man. The Bible says that God hates the proud. *"These six things doth the Lord hate: yea, seven are an abomination unto him: A proud look..."* (Proverbs 6:16-17)

We must develop a willing spirit to learn from anyone great and small in life. As long as the information is a relevant addition into our spiritual life we must embrace it with delight and with joy. It is written: *"The sacrifices of God are a broken spirit: a broken and a contrite heart, O God, thou wilt not despise."* (Psalms 51:17)

INTENSE STUDY OF THE WORD OF GOD

Study to shew thyself approved unto God,
a workman that needeth not to be ashamed,
rightly dividing the word of truth.
2 Timothy2:15

A deep and rich study of the word of God will provoke the giant inside of you to come alive. We must embrace searching and studying the scripture with clarity, precision, and wisdom. *"Till I come, give attendance to reading, to exhortation, to doctrine."* (1 Timothy 4:13)

FASTING & PRAYER

But thou, when thou prayest, enter into thy closet, and when thou hast shut thy door, pray to thy Father which is in secret; and thy Father which seeth in secret shall reward thee openly.
Matthew 6:6

But thou, when thou fastest, anoint thine head, and wash thy face; That thou appear not unto men to fast, but unto thy Father which is in secret: and thy Father, which seeth in secret, shall reward thee openly.
Matthew 17-18

Fasting and prayer is the gateway into His presence and in His presence is fulness of joy; at thy right hand there are pleasures for evermore. Prayer & fasting demands discipline, dedication, determination, and personal sacrifice. For anyone to develop spiritual muscles we must understand the mystery of prayer and fasting. We must develop the ability to hear from the throne room of God.

WE MUST BE SENSITIVE TO HEAR FROM GOD

It takes the understanding of how revelation gift of hearing and speaking to God works, for us to develop spiritual muscles in life. *"Who is blind, but my servant? or deaf, as my messenger that I sent? who is blind as he that is perfect, and blind as the Lord's servant? Seeing many things, but thou observest not; opening the ears, but he heareth not."* (Isaiah 42:19-20)

We must be sensitive to the voice of the spirit for us to develop spiritual muscles. *"But the natural man receiveth not the things of the Spirit of God: for they are foolishness unto him: neither can he know them, because they are spiritually discerned."* (1 Corinthians 2:14)

REPENT

Repentance is the pre-requisite to develop spiritual muscles. Until we are willing to repent we are not ready to develop spiritual muscles.

FAITH

"For whatsoever is born of God overcometh the world: and this is the victory that overcometh the world, even our faith." (1 John 5:4) It takes faith in God for us to develop spiritual muscles in life.

THE TRUTH ABOUT YOU

It is not an understatement when we say that you will not be here forever. At some point in our life we will eventually die. We must therefore invest our time in quality work, to make maximize our returns. Unless we embrace the truth, walk in the truth, live for the truth we will forever play the blame game life with our glorious destiny. Unless we take absolute responsibilities over every affairs of our lives, we will forever blame the devil and a third party. We must take time out to live a life, full of joy, praise, thanksgiving, honest, truthful reliable, responsible. etc.

Despite our background and differences we must be optimistic, and positive in life. Unless make eternity and success our only motive for living, crush all doubts and fear, we will never emerge winners in life. We must live a righteous life that must make an impact to our generation.

"To every thing there is a season, and a time to every purpose under the heaven: A time to be born, and a time to die; a time to plant, and a time to pluck up that which is planted; A time to kill, and a time to heal; a time to break down, and a time to build up; A time to weep, and a time to laugh; a time to mourn, and a time to dance; A time to cast away stones, and a time to gather stones together; a time to embrace, and a time to refrain from embracing; A time to get, and a time to lose; a time to keep, and a time to cast away; A time to rend, and a time to sew; a time to keep silence, and

a time to speak; A time to love, and a time to hate; a time of war, and a time of peace. What profit hath he that worketh in that wherein he laboureth? I have seen the travail, which God hath given to the sons of men to be exercised in it. He hath made every thing beautiful in his time: also he hath set the world in their heart, so that no man can find out the work that God maketh from the beginning to the end." (Ecclesiastes 3:1-11)

WE MUST GO IN-SEARCH OF WHAT THE WORD OF GOD IS SAYING CONCERNING OUR LIVES—soul, body, spirit, wealth & health

It is ignorant to be a Christian and nothing is moving and happening for us in our lives. Our God takes pleasure in our prosperity. Remember that scripture in Psalms 35:27— *"Let the Lord be magnified, which hath pleasure in the prosperity of his servant. We serve a rich God. It is written " The silver is mine, and the gold is mine, saith the Lord of hosts."* (Haggai 2:8)

Do you ever think God loves you poor? Oh no! God desire for us to be rich happy and content in life.

> *If ye then, being evil, know how to give good gifts*
> *unto your children, how much more shall*
> *your Father which is in heaven give*
> *good things to them that ask him?*
> **Matthew 7:11**

—God wants the best for us all in life. I tell you never settle for less in your life. Discover what is God's will concerning your life.

—God want us to dominate and be in authority in life. I say to you here never allow circumstances and worldly influential individual or groups of people to intimidate and make you feel inferior in life.

—God wants us to enjoy with pleasure every good and perfect thing , He made available for us in life.

—God want us to be happy in life. It is written godliness and contentment is great gain.

LOVE EVERYONE AND EVERYTHING AROUND YOUR LIFE

Owe no man anything, but to love one another: for he that loveth another hath fulfilled the law.
Romans 13:8

Remember…

Jesus said unto him, Thou shalt love the Lord thy God with all thy heart, and with all thy soul, and with all thy mind. This is the first and great commandment.
Matthew 22:37-38

For we can do nothing against the truth, but for the truth.
2 Corinthians 13:8

We must develop special skill and interest in the area of our calling.

What is the Lord saying about our calling in life?

For many are called, but few are chosen.
Matthew 22:14

Embrace your calling in life from God and begin to pursue it henceforth.

For I would that all men were even as I myself.
But every man hath his proper gift of God,
one after this manner, and another after that.
1 Corinthians 7:7

But as God hath distributed to every man,
as the Lord hath called every one, so let him walk.
And so ordain I in all churches.
1 Corinthians 7:17

Let every man abide in the same calling
wherein he was called.
1 Corinthians 7:20

Brethren, let every man, wherein he is called,
therein abide with God.
1 Corinthians 7:24

WE ARE CALLED WITH A HOLY CALLING

It is written—*"Who hath saved us, and called us with an holy calling, not according to our works, but according to his own purpose and grace, which was given us in Christ Jesus before the world began."* (2 Timothy 1:9)

WE ARE CALLED WITH DILIGENCE

Wherefore the rather, brethren,
give diligence to make your calling and election sure:
for if ye do these things, ye shall never fall.
2 Peter 1:10

It takes diligence to fulfil our calling in God. So many of us are off course and heading into the wrong direction. Every wrong direction leads into destruction. (See Proverbs 14:12 and Proverbs 16:25.) The truth is we are called in different discipline and areas of life. The truth is, we must identify what for us. We must identify our weakness and strength, threats and opportunities.

WHY MUST I TELL MYSELF THE TRUTH?

*And ye shall know the truth,
and the truth shall make you free.*
John 8:32

Often it is easy to live in denial for a prolong period of time in our lives. Perhaps we are plagued in object poverty, sickness and diseases or threats and assaults from demonic spirits Perhaps you lack money to pay your bills monthly or you do not have enough money/food or do not have a car. But you desire all these good things. What we are saying here is for you to tell yourself the truth.

WHAT ARE WE SAYING?

So many good Christians ended up in crooked business dealing, other good people are perishing in jail houses or dying of hunger and starvation. Not because it was the devil so to say but because they have lived in denial all through their youthful days. They have wasted all their precious time up to this time.

Examine yourselves, whether ye be in the faith.
2 Corinthians 13:5

Some addicted church folks will not work to make a living, simply because they do not take responsibility in life. If Jesus was all about hard work, what are we doing with idleness? *"But Jesus answered them, My Father worketh hitherto, and I work."* (John 5:17) We must take advantage of our God-given time in life. It is written—*"I must work the works of him that sent me, while it is day: the night cometh, when no man can work."* (John 9:4)

—Develop the consciousness and mentality not to quit in life

Winners in life never quit. So is also successful men/women in life. Unless we line up and position our life with what brings success in every area of our lives, we will forever remain in want of all things. We must be determined, dedicated, disciplined, make personal sacrifices and put in personal efforts for us to become outstanding and successful in life.

There is no food for the lazy man. As a believer, it is Christianity to engage our hand with meaningful work all the days of our lives.

Remember...

For even when we were with you, this we commanded you, that if any would not work, neither should he eat.
2 Thessalonians 3:10

OVERCOMERS MENTALITY

—Develop a winning mentality never to quit

Unless we develop the winning faith mentality, "if I perish, I perish," we will never obtain the riches and treasured reserved for heirs of God. *"For whatsoever is born of God overcometh the world: and this is the victory that overcometh the world, even our faith."* (1 John 5:4)

If you don't get any other revelation in this book, tell yourself the truth by embracing hard work as a lifestyle. *"Whatsoever thy hand findeth to do, do it with thy might; for there is no work, nor device, nor knowledge, nor wisdom, in the grave, whither thou goest."* (Ecclesiastes 9:10) Develop an optimistic consciousness and be positive about the outcome of your life. Trust in God and he will grant us our heart desire.

—Develop a breakthrough winning mentality

It is written—*"But the path of the just is as the shining light, that shineth more and more unto the perfect day."* (Proverbs 4:18)

There is nothing that is permitted to change around you, until you change your heart. Every great change in life, begins with a change of heart. Until you change your heart, you will forever remain the same.

HIS DESTINY WAS THE CROSS....

HIS PURPOSE WAS LOVE....

HIS REASON WAS YOU....

The wise prevail through great power, and those who have knowledge muster their strength shall never be ashamed.

Proverbs 24:5

PRAYER POINTS TO DEVELOP SPIRITUAL MUSCLES

—I destroy any spirit hindering my spiritual development, in the name of Jesus.

—I bind the spirit of fear intimidating in my life, in the name of Jesus.

—I break every demonic stronghold caging my life, in the name of Jesus.

—I command every spirit of terror of the night that is garaging my life and destiny, in the name of Jesus.

—You spirit of fear, loose your hold upon my life, in the name of Jesus.

—I paralyze all human agents using the spirits of fear to terrify me in the night to stumble and fall, in the name of Jesus.

—The fear and terror of the unbelievers shall not be my lot, in the name of Jesus.

—My tomorrow is blessed is Christ Jesus, therefore, you spirit that is responsible for the fear of tomorrow in my life, I bind you, in the name of Jesus.

—My destiny is attached to God, therefore I decree that I can never fail, in the name of Jesus.

—Every bondage that I am subjecting myself to by the spirit of fear, I break you, in the name of Jesus.

—All negative doors that the spirit of fear has opened in the past, be closed now, in the name of Jesus.

—Every disease, oppression and depression that came into my life as a result of fear, disappear now, in the name of Jesus.

—I refuse to be intimidated by any demonic nightmare, in the name of Jesus.

—Every enchantment and invocation of fear being made against me, I neutralize you and I command you to fail, in the name of Jesus.

—Every confederacy of the enemies in my home with the enemies outside shall not stand, in the name of Jesus.

—All arrangements of the devil concerning my home shall not stand; neither shall they come to pass, in the name of Jesus.

—I destroy all efforts of the enemy to frustrate my work, in the name of Jesus.

—I nullify every writing, agreement or covenant against my work, in the name of Jesus.

—Father Lord, increase my greatness and comfort me on every side, in the name of Jesus.

—O Lord, as You delight in my prosperity, I pray that You bless me in my work.

—Let no household enemy be able to control my well-being any longer, in the name of Jesus.

—Let all those who are against me without a cause in my place of work turn back and be brought to confusion, in the name of Jesus.

—I close every door through which the enemies have been working against my work, in the name of Jesus.

—No weapon of satan and his agents fashioned against me shall prosper, in the name of Jesus.

—My life is hid with Christ in God, therefore nobody can kill me or harm me, in the name of Jesus.

—I open wide all doors leading to my blessings, victory and breakthroughs which the enemies have closed, in the name of Jesus.

—Let all territorial spirit working against us in our neighborhood die, in the name of Jesus.

—Let every power contrary to the power of God operating to suppress people in my area be neutralized, in the name of Jesus.

—I bind every spirit of fear in my environment, in the name of Jesus.

—I destroy by fire every blockage harassing my life, in the name of Jesus.

—I bind every spirit of confusion in my life, in the name of Jesus.

—I reject failure over my life and assignment, in the name of Jesus.

—I nullify all strongholds caging my destiny, in the name of Jesus.

—I destroy all hindering spirits caging my life, in the name of Jesus.

—Holy Spirit, help my weakness, in the name of Jesus.

—O Lord, reveal your secret into greatness, in the name of Jesus.

—Father Lord, help me develop spiritually with speed, in the name of Jesus.

CHAPTER 1

The Lifestyle of Fasting & Prayer

But thou, when thou prayest, enter into thy closet, and when thou hast shut thy door, pray to thy Father which is in secret; and thy Father which seeth in secret shall reward thee openly.
Matthew 6:6

Fasting and prayer is the gateway into His Presence and Power. For anyone to develop spiritual muscles. We must be willing to pray and to fast often. Prayer and Fasting is so vital that it grants strength to our spiritual muscles. Just like as physical exercise develops our muscles, prayer and fasting puts strength to our spirits.

O thou that hearest prayer, unto thee shall all flesh come.
Psalms 65:2

The good news about fasting and prayer is that God records whatever is said per time for us all at any time. Prayer and fasting humbles us before the Almighty God who sees in the secret. Prayer and fasting pulls down our flesh, but lifts up our spirit. Remember… The devil operates easily with our flesh. Every time you fast and pray, you hinder the devil from arresting your flesh. That is why during prayer and fasting it is easy to get inspiration from the Holy Spirit. It is written—"For we wrestle not against flesh and blood..." (Ephesians 6:12)

Fasting and prayer is an avenue to harmonize our spirit directly with the spirit of God. Speedy answers is guaranteed whenever we pray and fast. Fasting and Prayer accelerates divine intervention from the Holy Ghost.

Likewise the Spirit also helpeth our infirmities:
for we know not what we should pray for as we ought:
but the Spirit itself maketh intercession for us
with groanings which cannot be uttered.
Romans 8:26

Our spiritual nature only develops through fasting and prayer. We must therefore discipline our flesh if we prayer and fasting must become our life style. Some folks only fast and pray when their pastor or Bishop ask them to fast and pray. Other only fast when going for a medical checkup as prescribed by their medical physician. We must all engraft prayer and fasting as a lifestyle if we must make an impact in our life time.

Prayer and fasting is significant and inevitable for anyone who desires to develop spiritual muscles. We must all learn how to pray and fast.

*And it came to pass, that, as he was praying
in a certain place, when he ceased,
one of his disciples said unto him, Lord,
teach us to pray, as John also taught his disciples.
And he said unto them, When ye pray, say,
Our Father which art in heaven,
Hallowed be thy name. Thy kingdom come.
Thy will be done, as in heaven, so in earth.
Give us day by day our daily bread.
And forgive us our sins; for we also forgive
every one that is indebted to us.
And lead us not into temptation;
but deliver us from evil*
Luke 11:1-4

It has been proven that everyone with a prayer and fasting life prevails against any temptation in life. Trials and temptation will come in life but as long as we have a prayer and fasting life, we easily prevail against it. *"There hath no temptation taken you but such as is common to man: but God is faithful, who will not suffer you to be tempted above that ye are able; but will with the temptation also make a way to escape, that ye may be able to bear it."* (1 Corinthians 10:13)

PRAYER & FASTING IS A COMMANDMENT OF GOD

"Is not this the fast that I have chosen? to loose the bands of wickedness, to undo the heavy burdens, and to let the oppressed go free, and that ye break every yoke?" (Isaiah 58:6)

"Moreover when ye fast, be not, as the hypocrites, of a sad countenance: for they disfigure their faces that they may appear unto men to fast. Verily I say unto you, They have their reward. But thou, when thou fastest, anoint thine head, and wash thy face; That thou appear not unto men to fast, but unto thy Father which is in secret: and thy Father, which seeth in secret, shall reward thee openly." (Matthew 6:16-18)

Our spiritual walk is not perfected without the incorporation of prayer and fasting as our lifestyle. It is mandatory for every believer who truly long to see His Power. The Holy Bible recommended us to pray and Fast as long as we live.

We must therefore embrace prayer and fasting as a lifestyle because it is a commandment of God. *"For this is the love of God, that we keep his commandments: and his commandments are not grievous."* (1 John 5:3)

EVERY TIME WE PRAY & FAST WE LAY UP TREASURES IN HEAVEN

"But lay up for yourselves treasures in heaven, where neither moth nor rust doth corrupt, and where thieves do not

break through nor steal: For where your treasure is, there will your heart be also." (Matthew 6:20-21)

Among other recommended ways to lay up treasure in heaven in the Bible is the place of prayer and fasting. It is good be a cheerful giver and to do good to all that come around you. To help the poor and the orphans. To promote peace and live a righteous lifestyle. But if you do all this and eliminate prayer and fasting, you miss out on some vital heavenly treasures. Without prayer and fasting as a lifestyle you subject your life vulnerable to the devil's attack.

PRAYER AND FASTING GRANTS US CONFIDENCE

As we develop a lifestyle of prayer and fasting, we secure heavenly confidence. Our mind is at peace concerning the prevailing challenges. We are relieved every time we consciously pray and fast concerning any obstacle or prevailing challenges in life. Prayer and fasting gives us assurance that God has heard our cry and our supplication. *"When I cry unto thee, then shall mine enemies turn back: this I know; for God is for me."* (Psalms 56:9)

THE DYNAMICS OF FASTING

The good news about prayer and fasting is that it convicts our spirit man that help and answer is on the way. Every time we consciously fast we are relieved of that prevailing predicament. When Daniel fasted for twenty one days an angel of God responded with an answer and told Daniel— *"thy words were heard, and I am come for thy words."* (Daniel 10:12)

Then said he unto me, Fear not, Daniel:
for from the first day that thou didst set
thine heart to understand, and to chasten thyself
before thy God, thy words were heard,
and I am come for thy words.
Daniel 10:12

ONE DAY FASTING

Then all the children of Israel, and all the people,
went up, and came unto the house of God, and wept,
and sat there before the Lord, and fasted that day
until even, and offered burnt offerings and peace
offerings before the Lord.
Judges 20:26

The same way you fast for a whole day to see your physician for a particular procedure, that is the same way we go before the Lord in fasting and prayer from early morning until evening to seek His face for answer. With the above scripture inline you will understand that a day fast is approved by the Holy Bible.

ABSOLUTE THREE DAYS OF FASTING

And he was three days without sight,
and neither did eat nor drink.
Acts 9:9

Go, gather together all the Jews that are
present in Shushan, and fast ye for me,
and neither eat nor drink three days, night or day:
I also and my maidens will fast likewise;
and so will I go in unto the king,
which is not according to the law:
and if I perish, I perish.
Esther 4:16

We are encouraged not to eat nor to drink in absolute fasting. Anyone seeking rapid and speedy answer from the Lord must engage in absolute three days of fasting & prayer with sincerity. Every time we fast without prayer, it is not fasting. It is called hunger strike. Fasting must be mixed with persistent intercession and supplication before God. We must pray from our spirit man until we get our desired answer.

TWENTY ONE DAYS OF FASTING

In those days I Daniel was mourning three full weeks.
I ate no pleasant bread, neither came flesh nor wine in
my mouth, neither did I anoint myself at all, till three
whole weeks were fulfilled.
Daniel 10:2-3

These days most churches begins the year with this fasting method, others do the forty days fasting which Jesus and Elijah did in the bible. Every time you are interceding for your community, or a national crisis or for a country we are encouraged to engage in a twenty one days of fasting and prayers.

BIBLE CHARACTERS THAT DEVELOPED SPIRITUAL MUSCLES BY FASTING

MOSES

*"And he was there with the Lord forty days and forty nights; he did neither eat bread, nor drink water. And he wrote upon the tables the words of the covenant, the Ten Commandments." (*Exodus 34:28)

Moses, the greatest prophet that ever lived, fasted for eighty days. This fasting secured not only the ten commandment but released the children of Israel from their Egyptians bondage.

APOSTLE PAUL

"In weariness and painfulness, in watchings often, in hunger and thirst, in fastings often, in cold and nakedness." (2 Corinthians 11:27)

The power behind Apostle Paul's ministry was fasting and total dedication to the things of God.

DANIEL

"In those days I Daniel was mourning three full weeks. I ate no pleasant bread, neither came flesh nor wine in my mouth, neither did I anoint myself at all, till three whole weeks were fulfilled." (Daniel 10:2-3)

Daniel although did no known miracle in his days, prevailed and witnessed four presidents come and go was because of his fasting and prayer life. The reason behind the excellent spirit was because Daniel was a man of fasting.

QUEEN ESTHER

"Go, gather together all the Jews that are present in Shushan, and fast ye for me, and neither eat nor drink three days, night or day: I also and my maidens will fast likewise; and so will I go in unto the king, which is not according to the law: and if I perish, I perish." (Esther 4:16)

Queen Esther prevailed and did not perish because of this three days of fasting and prayers.

JESUS

"And when he had fasted forty days and forty nights, he was afterward an hungred." (Matthew 4:2)

Jesus, to prevail against the devil temptation, humbled himself to the death because of this fast.

SUMMARY OF CHAPTER ONE

For us all to develop physical strength in life, we exercise our body daily. Apostle Paul said—*"And herein do I exercise myself, to have always a conscience void to offence toward God, and toward men."* (Acts 24:16)

We must embrace quality spiritual exercise by praying and fasting. We must embrace the power of God in praying and fasting in life. We must consciously watch and guide our heart from all inward sin.

We must embrace righteousness as a lifestyle. In my search I discovered that prayer and fasting as a lifestyle enhances spiritual growth, and also corporate growth of our ministries.

CHAPTER 2

INTENSE STUDY OF THE WORD OF GOD

*Study to shew thyself approved unto God,
a workman that needeth not to be ashamed,
rightly dividing the word of truth.*
2 Timothy 2:15

With my own little experience, no man or woman of God can develop spiritual strength without an intense diligent study of the word of God. Unless you know what is written, you will be written off *"...the sword of the Spirit, which is the word of God."* (Ephesians 6:17)

We must embrace an intense study of the word of God. A deep study of the word grants us spiritual sword to withstand and fight against the enemy. *"And take the helmet of salvation, and the sword of the Spirit, which is the word of God."* (Ephesians 6:17) Every time we are filled with the word of God the devil stays far away from us.

"And that from a child thou hast known the holy scriptures, which are able to make thee wise unto salvation through faith which is in Christ Jesus." (2 Timothy 3:15)

The study of the word of God makes us wise in life. As long as we align our lives according the holy commandments in scriptures, we have positioned our-

selves to prosper and to be successful in life.
Remember…

> *All scripture is given by inspiration of God,*
> *and is profitable for doctrine, for reproof,*
> *for correction, for instruction in righteousness:*
> *That the man of God may be perfect,*
> *thoroughly furnished unto all good works.*
> **2 Timothy 3:16-17**

First, the Word of God is an instrument of correction. It is easy for us to do our own things, even as the ministry is growing. It is easy to err. *"And Jesus answering said unto them, Do ye not therefore err, because ye know not the scriptures, neither the power of God?"* (Mark 12:24)

Mathew account puts it this way…

"Jesus answered and said unto them, Ye do err, not knowing the scriptures, nor the power of God." (Matthew 22:29)

"Every word of God is pure; He is a shield to those who put their trust in Him." The word of God corrects our lives from error, sin and destruction of the devil.

Second, the word of God is an instrument of instruction. It is written—*"I will instruct thee and teach thee in the way which thou shalt go: I will guide thee with mine eye."* (Pslams 32:8) We secured direction and profiting in life only through the word of God. *"Thus saith the Lord, thy Redeemer, the Holy One of Israel; I am the Lord thy God which teacheth thee to profit, which leadeth thee by the way that thou shouldest go."* (Isaiah 48:17) An intense study and practice of the word of God will make us outstanding in all things in life.

Third, the word of God is creative and innovative. It is written...

"By the word of the Lord were the heavens made; and all the host of them by the breath of his mouth." (Pslams 33:6) Oftentimes we seek for secular knowledge in the wrong place. Unless we embrace the word of God, we will never see divine wisdom produce in our lives.

Fourth, God's word is prophetic and totally sufficient for all of our needs. And God said—*"Let there be light: and there was light."* (Genesis 1:3)

2 Timothy 3:16-17 reads—*"All Scripture is given by inspiration of God, and is profitable for doctrine, for reproof, for correction, for instruction in righteousness, that the man of God may be complete, thoroughly equipped for every good work."* A greater responsibility as a Christian is to constantly study our bible and look for the truth. *"These were more noble than those in Thessalonica, in that they received the word with all readiness of mind, and searched the scriptures daily, whether those things were so."* (Acts 17:11)

Every time we deepened our study of the word, we develop readymade spiritual muscles to prevail against the adversary—the devil. Unless we constantly fill our heart and mind with the knowledge of the Holy Scriptures, we remain vulnerable and weak for the devil.

And fifth, the Word of God is power. *"For the kingdom of God is not in word, but in power."* (1 Corinthians 4:20)

It is written…

"For the word of God is quick, and powerful, and sharper than any twoedged sword, piercing even to the dividing asunder of soul and spirit, and of the joints and marrow, and is a discerner of the thoughts and intents of the heart." (Hebrews 4:12)

Every time we develop ourselves in the word of God, we gain power for dominion and authority in life. The word of God will accomplish what it promises. Whatever promises you discover from the Bible, use it to pray according to His will, He will grant it to you. Isaiah 55:11 says, *"So shall My word be that goes forth from My mouth; It shall not return to Me void, But it shall accomplish what I please, And it shall prosper in the thing for which I sent it."*

A wise man is strong;
yea, a man of knowledge increaseth strength.
Proverbs 24:5

For us all to make an impact in the kingdom of God we must develop and intense study of the word of God. *"As newborn babes, desire the sincere milk of the word that ye may grow thereby."* (1 Peter 2:2)

We must develop a quality intake of the word of God for spiritual strength and knowledge in all things. We increase in strength, in faith and in might by the knowledge of the word of God. *"If thou faint in the day of adversity, thy strength is small."* (Proverbs 24:10)

This I say then, *"Walk in the Spirit, and ye shall not fulfil the lust of the flesh."* (Galatians 5:17)

An intense quality word intake and word practice is the flat form to develop genuine spiritual strength. Even a dummy who takes their time to diligently develop qualitative intake of the word of God must grow in the knowledge of our Lord Jesus Christ. The Word says—*"As newborn babes, desire the sincere milk of the word, that ye may grow thereby:"* (1 Peter 2:2) It is written—*"According as his divine power hath given unto us all things that pertain unto life and godliness, through the knowledge of him that hath called us to glory and virtue."* (2 Peter 1:3)

If we live in the Spirit, let us also walk in the Spirit.
Galatians 2:25

It is our knowledge of the word of God that is the flat form to live in the spirit. Unless we carefully and diligently study the word of God, we will never operate in the realms of the spirit. We must therefore read our bible daily. It is written—*"All scripture is given by inspiration of God, and is profitable for doctrine, for reproof, for correction, for instruction in righteousness: That the man of God may be perfect, thoroughly furnished unto all good works."* (2 Timothy 3:16)

PRAYER POINTS TO DEVELOP SPIRITUAL STRENGTH

—I command every satanic hindrance against my rising, scattered to, in the name of Jesus.

—Holy Spirit, help my weakness, strength me, in the mighty name of Jesus

—I command and destroy every weapon fashion against me, in the name of Jesus.

—Holy Spirit of God, anoint me to pull down all negative strongholds hindering my spiritual life, in the name of Jesus.

—Let the fire of God strike down all demonic strongholds and mountains, militating against me, in the name of Jesus.

—Fire of God, anoint me with power to pursue, overtake and recover my stolen properties from the enemy.

—Every evil counsel against must come to naught, in the mighty name of Jesus.

—I destroy all stronghold of the devil against in my life, in Jesus's name.

—I cage all satanic coffins ganging up against me, in the name of Jesus.

—I command and destroy all stronghold harassing my finances, in Jesus's name.

—I paralyze every family stronghold caging my life and destiny, in the mighty name of Jesus.

—I break forth by the blood of Jesus. I plead the blood for victory over all satanic harassment, torture and intimidation, in the mighty name of Jesus.

—I receive the power of God to dominate, to pursue every stubborn power, to destroy every demonic stronghold, in the mighty name of Jesus.
—I develop faith to crust the enemy, in the mighty name of Jesus.
—O Lord, grant me spiritual power and might in the order of Samson to dominate all my oppressors, in the mighty name of Jesus
—Hand of God, roll me into unstoppable victory in life over every challenges and obstacles, in the mighty name of Jesus
—I destroy and overtake by forces, and by violence every stolen goods, inheritances that the devil has stolen from me, in the mighty name of Jesus.

SUMMARY OF CHAPTER TWO

A heavy and intense intake of the Word of God is the platform to develop spiritual strength. We must know what the word of God is saying concerning every issue in life. "If you do not know what is written, you will be written off." We must discover what is written concerning us, we must embrace and activate the promises of God concerning our life by studying our bible daily.

—Take time to search the scripture for the word is power.
—A deep study of the word will grant you access into His power.
—Knowing the word is knowing God.
—Unless you know what is written, you will be written off.
—Unless we develop a quality intake of the word we remain vulnerable to the devil.
—Study the word to show our self-approved.
—The word is the path way instruction and revelation in all things
—The word is the gateway in to His presence, and in His presence in His presence is fulness of joy; at thy right hand there are pleasures for evermore.
—As long as you desire to develop spiritual muscles, take time out to develop in your knowledge of the word of God.

CHAPTER 3

UNDERSTANDING MENTORSHIP

That ye be not slothful, but followers of them who through faith and patience inherit the promises.
Hebrews 6:12

The American Heritage College Dictionary defined a mentor as a wise and trusted counselor or teacher. As long as we live we must understand the role model of a mentor. Mentor are teachers who shape our behavior and lifestyle. Mentors are short cut into developing spiritual muscles. Every mentor always passes His/her anointing on the mentee.

BIBLICAL MENTORS THAT PASSED THEIR ANNOINTING TO THEIR MENTEE

MOSES THE MENTOR

Talking about Moses the Bible said—*"And there arose not a prophet since in Israel like unto Moses, whom the Lord knew face to face."* (Deuteronomy 34:10) *"And by a prophet the Lord brought Israel out of Egypt, and by a prophet was he preserved."* (Hosea 12:13)

MOSES MENTORED JOSHUA IN THE BIBLE

The fame and might of Joshua who came from the tribe of Ephraim, was not only due to his family background. But Joshua might spread all round the region because one of the greatest prophet that ever lived mentored him. *"And Joshua the son of Nun was full of the spirit of wisdom; for Moses had laid his hands upon him: and the children of Israel hearkened unto him, and did as the Lord commanded Moses."* (Deuteronomy 34:9)

ELIJAH MENTORED ELISHA IN THE BIBLE

Elisha was able to performed 32 miracles in his lifetime because His mentor who performed only 16 miracles in His life time anointed him with a double portion of the mantle he carried. *"He took up also the mantle of Elijah that fell from him, and went back, and stood by the bank of Jordan; And he took the mantle of Elijah that fell from him, and smote the waters, and said, Where is the Lord God of Elijah? and when he also had smitten the waters, they parted hither and thither: and Elisha went over."* (2 Kings 2:13-14)

JESUS MENTORED US ALL AND THE 12 DISCIPLES

"Then he called his 12 disciples together, and gave them power and authority over all devils, and

to cure diseases. And he sent them to preach the kingdom of God, and to heal the sick." (Luke 9:1-2)

Mentors are role models we look up to in life. ***"Without a mentor, we are left to the tormentor."***

WHAT DOES THAT MEAN, YOU MAY ASK?

Without Jesus in our lives, we are left to the tormentor. Jesus gave us His principles to model our lives. Jesus gave us his fundamental rule and greatest commandment to love everyone as our selves. Besides the name of Jesus are the principles of Jesus to approach complex life challenging issues.

As long as we receive Jesus, we secured His power. *"But as many as received him, to them gave he power to become the sons of God, even to them that believe on his name."* (John 1:12)

And be not conformed to this world:
but be ye transformed by the renewing of your mind,
that ye may prove what is that good, and acceptable,
and perfect, will of God.
Romans 12:2

As we all know the devil easily attacks our mind with fear. For all spiritual muscles development are of the mind. We must diligently guide our mind. *"Keep thy heart with all diligence; for out of it are the issues of life."* (Proverbs 4:23) *"And be re-*

newed in the spirit of your mind." (Ephesians 4:23)

We develop faith to confront the enemy in the mind. *"For whatsoever is born of God overcometh the world: and this is the victory that overcometh the world, even our faith. Who is he that overcometh the world, but he that believeth that Jesus is the Son of God?"* (1 John 5:4-5)

APOSTLE PAUL MENTORED TIMOTHY

Although mentoring relationship has received a great worldwide attention from both secular and organizational leadership researchers and leadership practitioners alike. All noted progressive mentoring relationships result in benefits to the protégé.

Apostle Paul demonstrated the value of developing Timothy his spiritual son into a more efficient and effective leader. Paul carefully selected Timothy to work with him in the ministry, equipped him for ministerial tasks, empowered him for success, employed him in a challenging work environment, and communicated to Timothy the value of their relationship.

HINDRACE TO MENTORSHIP

PRIDE

*Pride goeth before destruction,
and an haughty spirit before a fall.*
Proverbs 16:18

We must always watch out for pride in our life. For us to be properly mentored we must be humble willing to learn and open to receive new information and revelation and also ready to ask relevant questions.

IGNORANT

Lest Satan should get an advantage of us: for we are not ignorant of his devices.
2 Corinthians 2:11

Ignorance will lead us into destruction. we must all embrace the truth of the word of God *"But if ye refuse and rebel, ye shall be devoured with the sword: for the mouth of the Lord hath spoken it."* (Isaiah 1:20)

All stubborn and disobedient people will never accept the concept of a mentor in their life. But as long as you are living in disobedience you will always suffer frustration because of lack of a mentor and a coach in your life.

UNWILLING TO LEARN

Some of us will never learn from nobody, because we lack the spirit to learn from anybody. An unwilling spirit to learn will hinder us from mentorship. And as long as we are not open to learning, to embrace ideas from experienced people, we will never grow in life.

ACCESS INTO THE SUPERNATURAL

BE BORN AGAIN
We must be born again for us to experience the supernatural and mentorship.

THE FEAR OF GOD
"The fear of the Lord is the beginning of wisdom: and the knowledge of the holy is understanding." (Proverbs 9:10) We must respect, revere and fear God.

RIGHTEOUS LIFESTYLE
We must live a righteous, and a moral life free of accusation. It is written—*"And Paul, earnestly beholding the council, said, Men and brethren, I have lived in all good conscience before God until this day. .And herein do I exercise myself, to have always a conscience void to offence toward God, and toward men."* (Acts 24:16)

INTEGRITY

The integrity of the upright shall guide them.
Proverbs 11:3

Talking about David, the Bible says, *"So he fed them according to the integrity of his heart; and guided them by the skillfulness of his hands."* (Psalms 78:72) It is written, *"A good name is rather to be chosen than great riches, and loving favour rather than silver and gold."* We are not guaranteed to experience the supernatural until we exhibit integrity as a character.

SOUL WINNING

It is written, *"And he that winneth souls is wise."* (Proverbs 11:30) Soul winning is the gateway into the supernatural. We must evangelize and speak to all that come our way about the Lord Jesus.

What must I do to become a born again Christian?

You must be born again!

The Word says as many as received him, to them gave He power to become the sons of God. Even to them that believe on His name. To qualify for divine visitation, do the following sincerely:

1) Acknowledge that you are a sinner and that He died for you. (Romans 3:23)

2) Repent of your sins. (Acts 3:19, Luke 13:5, 2 Peter 3:9)

3) Believe in your heart that Jesus died for your sin. (Romans 10:10)

4) Confess Jesus as the Lord over your life. (Romans 10:10, Acts 2:21)

Chapter 3   Understanding Mentorship

Now repeat this prayer after me:

*"Say Lord Jesus, I accept you today, as my Lord and my savior, forgive me of my sins, wash me with your blood. Right now, I believe, I am sanctified, I am saved, I am free, I am free from the power of sin to serve the Lord Jesus.
Thank you Lord for saving me. Amen."*

Congratulations.

YOU ARE NOW A BORN AGAIN CHRISTIAN!

AGAIN I SAY TO YOU...

CONGRATULATIONS!

WE MUST DEAL WITH EVERY INWARD SIN THAT HINDERS OUR PRAYERS

Godly wisdom demand that we learn and understand how to relate and interact with each other husband and wife through the help of the word of God. It is written—*"Likewise, ye husbands, dwell with them according to knowledge, giving honour unto the wife, as unto the weaker vessel, and as being heirs together of the grace of life; that your prayers be not hindered."* (1 Peter 3:7)

Remember...

"Submitting yourselves one to another in the fear of God. Wives, submit yourselves unto your own husbands, as unto the Lord. For the husband is the head of the wife, even as Christ is the head of the church: and he is the saviour of the body." (Ephesians 5:21-23)

"Husbands, love your wives, even as Christ also loved the church, and gave himself for it." (Ephesians 5:25)

"So ought men to love their wives as their own bodies. He that loveth his wife loveth himself." (Ephesians 5:28)

WE MUST BE DELIVERED FROM EVERY BITTERNESS OF THE HEART

It is written—*"Looking diligently lest any man fail of the grace of God; lest any root of bitterness springing up trouble you, and thereby many be defiled."* (Hebrews 12:15) We must prove our moral citizenship by the way we live and deal with everyone around us. It is written—*"Blessed are the peacemakers: for they shall be called the children of God."* (Matthew 5:9)

WE MUST ALL REPENT OF EVERY SIN THAT EASILY BESET US

It is written—*"...not willing that any should perish, but that all should come to repentance."* (2 Peter 3:9)

As spiritual people we must cultivate the consciousness of eternity. There are a lot of people that live and do things like they do not have conscience. To really develop spiritual strength we must first develop the following:

WE MUST BE PURE IN OUR HEARTS

It is written—*"Blessed are the pure in heart: for they shall see God."* (Matthew 5:8) God will not protect and defend us in the day of adversity if our heart is defiled. We must therefore purify our conscience from all evil and dead works, thoughts, and actions. Every evil heart and conscience manifests diabolic strength, produces evil work of the devil. *"Unto the pure all things are pure: but unto them that are defiled and unbelieving is nothing pure; but even their mind and conscience is defiled."* (Titus 1:15)

Remember...

"How much more shall the blood of Christ, who through the eternal Spirit offered himself without spot to God, purge your conscience from dead works to serve the living God?" (Hebrews 9:14)

WE MUST PRACTICE RIGHTEOUSNESS

Blessed are they which do hunger and thirst after righteousness: for they shall be filled.
Matthew 5:6

Unless we embrace righteousness as a lifestyle, developing spiritual muscles and strength is not guaranteed by the hand of God. Righteousness is a virtue that we must embrace as a lifestyle if we must walk in strength, in power and in authority. It is written—"... he that doeth righteousness is righteous, even as he is righteous." (1 John 3:7)

WE MUST BE PEACEMAKERS

The angels of the Living God protect, defend and vindicate every true peace maker in life. As peacemaker, our Lord Jesus Christ advocates and defends us against every tribulation, trial, court case and family matter. Also, the Lord Jesus fights for us agains prevailing challenges and conflicts of life. The Almighty God will release spiritual muscles, power and strength when we make ourselves peacemakers in life. *"Blessed are the peacemakers: for they shall be called the children of God."* (Matthew 5:9)

WE MUST BE MERCIFUL

The acts of mercy is a virtue that comes from the heart of every believer. As believers we must prove the dignity of our Christianity by showing mercy to all. Until we learn and embrace the act of showing mercy to others we will not gain genuine strength, power, and authority in life. *"Blessed are the merciful: for they shall obtain mercy."* (Matthew 5:7)

WE MUST LOVE OUR NEIGHBORS AS OURSELVES

Unless we develop our love for God and for others around our lives, we will never be able to develop genuine power and authority to dominate the devil. It is written—*"For love is strong as death."* (Songs of Solomon 8:6)

Remember...

"For God so loved the world, that he gave his only begotten Son, that whosoever believeth in him should not perish, but have everlasting life." (John 3:16) God expects us to show love from a genuine heart to everyone around us. Jesus said, *"Thou shalt love thy neighbour as thyself."* (Matthew 22:39) *"And we have known and believed the love that God hath to us. God is love; and he that dwelleth in love dwelleth in God, and God in him."* (1 John 4:16)

WE MUST BE MEEK IN LIFE

God does not release His power to any proud man/woman. Until we are humbled and meek in life, we will never experience His presence that comes with fullness of joy. Remember that at His right hand is pleasures for us all for evermore. One of the greatest secret of Moses greatness was hidden in meekness. It is written—*"Now the man Moses was very meek, above all the men which were upon the face of the earth."* (Numbers 12:3)

MEEKNESS MADE MOSES THE GREATEST

"And there arose not a prophet since in Israel like unto Moses, whom the Lord knew face to face," (Deuteronomy 34:10)

We must genuinely examine our lives if we honestly desire to develop spiritual muscles, strength, power, authority to dominate the wicked one.

Remember...

Examine yourselves, whether ye be in the faith; prove your own selves. Know ye not your own selves, how that Jesus Christ is in you, except ye be reprobates?
2 Corinthians 13:5

We must consciously do away with every outward sin in our lives. The book of Galatian summarized for us all outward sin in life.

"Now the works of the flesh are manifest, which are these; Adultery, fornication, uncleanness, lasciviousness, Idolatry, witchcraft, hatred, variance, emulations, wrath, strife, seditions, heresies, Envyings, murders, drunkenness, revellings, and such like: of the which I tell you before, as I have also told you in time past, that they which do such things shall not inherit the kingdom of God." (Galatians 5:20-22)

HOW TO I COME OUT OF SIN?

It is written—*"...Repent, and be baptized every one of you in the name of Jesus Christ for the remission of sins, and ye shall receive the gift of the Holy Ghost."* (Acts 2:38)

To come out of sin first, we must repent. Repentance is the first step into healing and deliverance. We will never experience genuine power and encounter His presence unless we genuinely repent of our sins. *"If we confess our sins, he is faithful and just to forgive us our sins, and to cleanse us from all unrighteousness."* (1 John 1:9)

WHENEVER WE REPENT WE POSITION OURSELVES TO RECEIVE POWER

"But as many as received him, to them gave he power to become the sons of God, even to them that believe on his name." (John 1:12)

WE MUST CONFESS JESUS AS THE LORD OVER YOUR LIFE

We must confess with our mouth that Jesus is Lord. *"For with the heart man believeth unto righteousness; and with the mouth confession is made unto salvation."* (Romans 10:10)

We must engage in the following for spiritual muscles development:

ACKNOWLEDGE

We acknowledge we are all sinners, and that He died for our sake. (Romans 3:23)

WE MUST REPENT OF OUR SINS

We must repent of our sins. (Acts 3:19, Luke13:5, 2 Peter 3:9)

WE MUST BELIEVE IN GOD

We must believe in God for us to experience power, authority, and strength. *"But as many as received him, to them gave he power to become the sons of God, even to them that believe on his name."* (John 1:12)

HOW TO PROVOKE THE POWER OF THE HOLY GHOST

BELIEVE IN THE MINISTRY OF THE HOLY SPIRIT

For us to encounter the power and presence of the Holy Spirit, we must believe in Him and in His ministry.

1) **ACKNOWLEDGE** the person of the Holy Spirit.

2) **BELIEVE** in the ministration of the Holy Spirit

3) **SUBMIT & OBEY** the person of the Holy Spirit.

4) **WELCOME** the supernatural presence of the Holy Spirit.

Chapter 3   Understanding Mentorship

For everyone that desired the help of the Holy Spirit, divine wisdom demands that we develop a relationship with the person of the Holy Spirit. Every man of strength and power is a man/woman that operated under the influence of the Holy Spirit.

"Even the Spirit of truth; whom the world cannot receive, because it seeth him not, neither knoweth him: but ye know him; for he dwelleth with you, and shall be in you. I will not leave you comfortless: I will come to you." (John 14:17-18)

SUMMARY OF CHAPTER THREE

The approved short cut in life is through mentorship. Everyone who came under the tutelage of a mentor has a great advantage over those that never had a mentor in their life. Mentorship helps us develop quick experience in life. Mentorship is the idea of life, we put to use our skill and talent acquired from our master as mentees. Therefore everyone in search for spiritual strength development must first get a mentor they must follow in their life. There are mentors whom you will never meet in your lifetime, but we can look if they left any written materials. A great number of my mentors I never met during their lifetime. But I bought their books, studied their books and listened to their audio sermons. This practice help mold and shaped my own life in the gospel ministry. The great Late Oral Roberts, Kenneth Hagin, Tl Osborne, Benson Idahosa, I did not have the privilege at a time to meet them one on one, but I read almost all their books and it helped me greatly.

WHAT ARE WE SAYING?

Mentorship is the biblical principle for spiritual strength development. For every one seeking for His power and His presence, we shoiuld look for a role model in the area of our calling who will serve as our mentor and coach.

STAY WITH YOUR MENTOR
AS LONG AS GOD PERMITS YOU

Never say I have learned enough, let me launch out on my own unless the Lord Spirit released you on this wise. For us to develop genuine spiritual strength, we must spend time with our mentors. Joshua tarried with Moses. *"And Joshua the son of Nun, the servant of Moses, one of his young men, answered and said, My lord Moses, forbid them."* (Numbers 11:28) Elisha tarried with Elijah, Timothy stayed long with Apostle Paul.

DECISION KEYS

1) Nothing changes until you make up your mind.

2) Decision is the gateway to deliverance.

3) Until you decisde, no one will decisde for you.

4) Your prosperity is proportional to your decisions.

5) The decision you make will determine the future you will create.

6) Decision creates future and fulfills destinies.

7) Decision beautiflies our future.

8) Decision keeps you out of trouble.

9) Decision exempts you from evil.

10) Decision gurantees eternity.

11) You can only go far in life by your faith decisions.

12) You are poor because you made such decisions.

13) Make a decision and change your life.

14) Life changing decisions is a function of quality information.

15) Success in life is a function of decision.

16) Life experiences is full of decisions.

17) Decisions changes destinies.

18) Never settle for information, only look for revelation.

19) You are where you are today based on your last decision.

20) Information is crucial in decision making.

21) Decision makers rule the world.

22) You can rule your world by quality decisions.

23) As long as you decide rightly satan cannot harrass you.

CONDITION TO RECEIVE THE HOLY SPIRIT

REPENTANCE
Repent, and be baptized every one of you in the name of Jesus Christ for the remission of sins, and ye shall receive the gift of the Holy Ghost.

BE BAPTIZED
Be baptized every one of you in the name of Jesus Christ for the remission of sins, and ye shall receive the gift of the Holy Ghost.

CONFESS OF YOUR SIN
If we confess our sins, he is faithful and just to forgive us our sins, and to cleanse us from all unrighteousness.

ACKNOWLEDGMENT
Acknowledge that you are a sinner and that Jesus Christ died for your sins. (Romans 3:23)

BORN AGAIN
"Jesus answered and said unto him, Verily, verily, I say unto thee, Except a man be born again, he cannot see the kingdom of God." (John 3:3-8)

PRINCIPLES OF DIVINE CONNECTION

—Have faith in God.
—Believe in yourself.
—Always follow the footsteps of your mentors.
—Always carry a mental picture of your actual future.
—Live a righteous life.
—Keep company with the right people.
—Be willing to confront all your challenges/conflicts.
—Never give up in life.
—Be disciplined.
—Be dedicated.
—Be determined.
—Always make personal efforts and sacrifice.
—Depart from evil and learn to do well.

CONCLUSION

And I will restore to you the years that the locust hath eaten, the cankerworm, and the caterpiller, and the palmerworm, my great army which I sent among you.
Joel 2:25

Irrespective of how far you have gone in a wrong direction, you will never get to the destination. We are all called by God, but few are chosen. *"For many are called, but few are chosen."* (Matthew 22:14)

Chapter 3   Understanding Mentorship

Wherefore the rather, brethren,
give diligence to make your calling and election sure:
for if ye do these things, ye shall never fall.
2 Peter 1:9

Who hath saved us, and called us with an holy calling,
not according to our works, but according to
his own purpose and grace, which was given us
in Christ Jesus before the world began.
2 Timothy 1:10

Without purpose your life has no meaning. Every career is not for you, but there IS an assignment for your life.

For I would that all men were even as I myself.
But every man hath his proper gift of God,
one after this manner, and another after that.
1 Corinthians 7:7
But as God hath distributed to every man,
as the Lord hath called every one, so let him walk.
And so ordain I in all churches.
1 Corinthians 7:17

Let every man abide in the same calling
wherein he was called.
1 Corinthians 7:20

Brethren, let every man, wherein he is called,
therein abide with God.
1 Corinthians 7:24

God is willing to restore our lives, but you have a part to play in this relationship.

HAVE YOU DISCOVERED YOUR GIFT FROM GOD?

A man's gift maketh room for him, and bringeth him before great men.
Proverbs 18:16

Although God wants you to breakthrough in life, you have a greater role to play in this covenant relationship. Remember how Joseph's gift in the Bible brought him before the king? Daniel's gift in the Bible brought him before four presidents and kings.

Discover your talent from God and pursue it with all your might. You must recover your destiny in the mighty name of Jesus. Don't give up on your destiny because winners do not quit. Never waste any day of your life because your time is your money.

FAVOR CONFESSION

Father, thank you for making me righteous and accepted through the blood of Jesus Christ. Because of that, I am blessed and highly favored by God. I am the subject of your affection. Your favor surrounds me as a shield, and the first thing that people see around me is your favored shield.

Thank you that I have favor with you and man today. All day long people go out of their way to bless me and help me. I have favor with everyone that I deal with today. Doors that were once closed are now opened for me. I receive preferential treatment and I have special privileges. I am God's favored child.

No good thing will He withhold from me. Because of God's favor, my enemies cannot triumph over my life. I have supernatural increases and promotions. I declare restoration to everything that the devil has stolen from my life. I have honor in the midst of my adversaries and an increase in assets, especially in real estate and expansion of territories.

Because I am highly favored by God, I experience great victories, supernatural turnarounds and miraculous breakthroughs in the midst of great impossibilities. I receive recognition, prominence and honor. Petitions are granted to me even by ungodly authorities. Policies, rules, regulations and laws are changed and reversed on my behalf.

I win battles that I don't even have to fight, because God fights them for me. This is the day, the set time and the designated moment for me to experience the free favor of God that profusely and lavishly abounds on my behalf, in Jesus' name. Amen.

YOU MUST BE BORN AGAIN

If you are a born again Christian, we'd like to encourage you in your Christian life. If you are not a born again Christian, we can help you here receive genuine salvation. *"Therefore if any man be in Christ, he is a new creature: old things are passed away; behold, all things are become new."* (2 Corinthians 5:17)

Now repeat this prayer after me:

Say Lord Jesus, I accept you today, as my Lord and my savior, forgive me of my sins, wash me with your blood. Right now I believe, I am sanctified, I am saved, I am free, I am free from the power of sin to serve the Lord Jesus. Thank you, Lord, for saving me. Amen.

Congratulations...

YOU ARE NOW A BORN AGAIN CHRISTIAN!

How to I come out of sin?

It is written: *"Repent, and be baptized every one of you in the name of Jesus Christ for the remission of sins, and ye shall receive the gift of the Holy Ghost."* (Acts 2:38)

To come out of sin first, we must repent. Repentance is the first step into healing and deliverance. We will never experience genuine power and encounter His presence unless we genuinely repent of our sins. *"If we confess our sins, he is faithful and just to forgive us our sins, and to cleanse us from all unrighteousness."* (1 John 1:9)

Whenever we repent we position ourselves to receive power. *"But as many as received him, to them gave he power to become the sons of God, even to them that believe on his name."* (John 1:12)

We must confess Jesus as the Lord over your life. We must confess with our mouth that Jesus is Lord. *"For with the heart man believeth unto righteousness; and with the mouth confession is made unto salvation."* (Romans 10:10)

We must engage in the following for spiritual muscles development.

Acknowledge

We acknowledge we are all sinners, and that He died for our sake. (Romans 3:23)

We must repent of our sins

We must repent of our sins. (Acts 3:19, Luke 13:5, 2 Peter 3:9)

We must believe in God

We must believe in God for us to experience power, authority, and strength. *"But as many as received him, to them gave he power to become the sons of God, even to them that believe on his name."* (John 1:12)

How to provoke the Power of the Holy Ghost

Believe in the ministry of the Holy Spirit. For us to encounter the power and presence of the Holy Spirit, we must believe in Him and in His ministry.

1) Acknowledge the person of the Holy Spirt.

2) Believe in the ministration of the Holy Spirit.

3) Submit & obey the person of the Holy Spirit.

4) Welcome the supernatural presence of the Holy Spirit.

For everyone that desires the help of the Holy Spirit, divine wisdom demands that we develop a relationship with the person of the Holy Spirit. Every man of strength and power is a man/woman that operated under the influence of the Holy Spirit.
"Even the Spirit of truth; whom the world cannot receive, because it seeth him not, neither knoweth him: but ye know him; for he dwelleth with you, and shall be in you. I will not leave you comfortless: I will come to you." (John 14:17-18)

Chapter 3   Understanding Mentorship

WISDOM KEYS

—Every productive society is a society heading to the top.

—Millions of Nigerians run away from Nigeria. Very few Nigerians stay in Nigeria.

—My decision to return Nigeria is the will of God for my life.

—My shortcoming in America after 18 years is the fact that I've trained me to be wise, to think, reflect and reason appropriately.

—If you train your mind to reason, it will train your hands to earn money.

—It is absurd to use the money of the heathen to build the kingdom of the living God.

—Every ministry reveals its agenda and VISION either at the beginning or at the end.

—Be careful of your life. It is your first ministry.

—The average American mind is conditioned for a continual quest to get new things and discard the old.

—When I considered well, my BMW jeep became my initial deposit for the work of the ministry in Nigeria.

—Money will never fall from any tree or person. Make up your mind to be independent today.

—Everyone is waiting for you to change your mind. Until you change your thinking, nothing changes around you.

—Multiple academic degrees in other disciplines gave me the chance to think and reason.

—Whatever anyone is thinking at any time reveals what is inside of their heart.

—All planned events are the product of meditation.

—Every event is designed for a designated timeline.

—Wisdom is your ability to think, to create and invent.

— If you can think wisely enough, you will come out of debt.

—The distance between you and your success is your innovative and creative ability to think well.

—Success is the result of hard work, commitment, resolve and determined learning from past mistakes and failings.

—If you organize your mind, you have organized your

life and destiny.

—There is a thin line between success and failure.

—Wealth is your ability to think, power is your ability to reason and success is your ability to be informed.

—If you can make use of your mind by thinking and reasoning, God will make use of your life and destiny.

—Reflect, reason, think and be great.

—Famous people are born of woman.

—That you will make it is your intention, that you will survive is your resolve, that you will succeed with changes is your determination, personal efforts and hard work.

—No man was born a failure.

—Lack of vision is the result of failure.

—Working with mental patients encourages and aspire me to be a productive observant and dedicated to my assignment.

—Successful people are not magicians. It is the will-power, combined with hard work and determination and a resolve to succeed, that make them succeed.

—In the unequivocal state of the mind, intention is not a location or a position. It is the state of the mind.

—So many people think that they think. The mind is used to think, to reflect and to reason. You will remain blind with your eyes open until you can see with your mind by thinking.

—There is no favoritism in accurate and precise calculation.

—Although knowledge is power, information is the key and gateway to a great future.

—It will take the hand of God to move the hand of man.

—With the backing of the great wise God, nothing will disconnect you from your inheritance.

—As long as you have wisdom and understanding of God, Satan and evil cannot manipulate your life and destiny.

—You have come this far in life by your own judgment and the decisions you made in the past. Now lean in and listen to God for another dimension of greatness.

—Great people are ordinary people. It is extra ordinary efforts and the price of sacrifice that produces greatness in them.

—As a mental direct care worker, I saw a great pastor and a motivational speaker within myself.

—A menial job does not reduce your self-worth. Until you resolve to achieve greatness and see greatness in all you do, you will never count in your community.

—The principle of Jesus will solve your gambling and addiction problems.

—The man of Jesus will lead you into heaven.

—Everyone has their self-appraisal and what they think about you. Until you discover yourself, other opinions about you will alter the real you.

—Supervisors and directors are just a position in the chain of command in a workplace. Never allow your supervisor hierarchy to alter your opinion of yourself.

—Everyone can come out of debt if they make up their mind.

—The fact that I am not a decision-maker at work does not diminish my contribution to my world.

—Although it appears like it was a poor decision to accept a direct care employment at a psychiatric hospital, as I reflect on my nine years of that experience, it became apparent that I have learned and experienced enough for my next assignment.

—Self-encouragement and determination is a resolve of the heart.

—If you are determined to make a difference and do the things that make a difference, you will eventually make a difference.

—Good things do not come easy.

—Short cuts will cut your life short.

—Those who look ahead move ahead.

—Life is all about making an impact. In your lifetime strive to make an impact in your community.

—Make friends and connect with people who are moving ahead of you in life.

—If you can look around well, you have come a long way in your life, made a lot of difference and realized a lot of success in life.

—If you are my old friend, hurry up to reach out to me before I become a stranger to you.

—I am blessed with inspirations from God that changed my interpretation of the world around me.

—I thought I was stagnant and lonely until I looked around and noticed my children running around and my wife cooking.

—At 40, I resigned my job to seek the Lord forever.

—My ministry took a drastic rise to the top when the wisdom of God visited me with knowledge and understanding.

—You will be a better person if you understand the characteristics of your personality like your mood swings, attitudes and habits.

—It is the seed of love you sow into the heart of a child and a woman that you reap in due time.

—Love is not selfish. Love shares everything, including the concealed secrets of the mind.

—As long as you have a prayer life and a Bible, you will never feel lonely in the race of life.

—When good friends disconnect from you, let them go. They might have seen something new in a different direction.

—Confidence in yourself and in God is the only way to bring you out of captivity

—Never train a child to waste his or her time.

—The mind is the greatest asset of a great future.

—You walk by common sense, run by principles and fly by instruction.

—Those who become successful in life did it by self-determination, hard work and learning from past failures.

—Most successful people are lonely people. No one renders help to them, believing they are already successful. Except when they seek for more knowledge and information, they are all alone.

— I have seen a towing truck vehicle. I have also seen a towing ship in the water. But I have never seen a towing airplane in the air.

—I exercise my judgment and make a decision every minute of the day. Decisions are crucial, critical and vital with reference to your future.

—So many people wish for a great future. You can only work towards a great future.

—Your celebrity status began when you discovered

your talent. What are you good at? Work at it with all your commitment.

—Prayers will sustain you, but the wisdom of God will prosper you.

—When I met Oyedepo, his teachings changed my perspective. But when I met Ibiyeomie, his teachings changed my perception.

—I will be successful in ministry if only I concentrate and focus my energy in the work of the ministry.

—It took the late Dr. Norman Vincent Peale's book to open my mind towards the kingdom of success.

CHAPTER 4

PRAYER OF SALVATION

For with the heart man believeth unto righteousness; and with the mouth confession is made unto salvation.
Romans 10:10

In my understanding, salvation is a personal thing. We must develop quality time to fellowship with the Holy Spirit, and more also to develop a personal relationship with our Lord Jesus Christ. We are not safe until we are saved.

Neither is there salvation in any other: for there is none other name under heaven given among men, whereby we must be saved.
Acts 4:12

"And brought them out, and said, Sirs, what must I do to be saved? And they said, Believe on the Lord Jesus Christ, and thou shalt be saved, and thy house." (Acts 16:30-31)

To qualify for salvation, we must be born again! The Word says as many as received him, to them gave He power to become the sons of God. Even to them that believe on his name.

Chapter 4   Prayer of Salvation

To qualify for divine visitation, do the following with sincerity—

> 1) Acknowledge that you are a sinner and that He died for you. (Romans 3:23)
>
> 2) Repent of your sins. (Acts 3:19, Luke 13:5, 2 Peter 3:9)
>
> 3) Believe in your heart that Jesus died for your sins. (Romans 10:10)
>
> 4) Confess Jesus as the Lord over your life. (Romans 10:10, Acts 2:21)

Now repeat this prayer after me:

Say Lord Jesus, I accept you today, as my Lord and my savior. Forgive me of my sins, wash me with your blood. Right now, I believe I am sanctified, I am saved, I am free. I am free from the power of sin, to serve the Lord Jesus. Thank you Lord for saving me. Amen.

Congratulations. You are now...

A BORN AGAIN CHRISTIAN.

Again I say to you—CONGRATULATIONS!

I adjure you to watch the Spirit of God bear witness with your Spirit confirming His word with signs following. The Word says the Spirit itself beareth witness with our spirit, that we are the children of God.

MIRACLE CARE OUTREACH

"...But that the members should have the same care one for another"
1 Corinthians 12:25

We are all members of the body of Christ. Jesus commanded us to love our neighbor as ourselves. This includes caring for one another as a member of one body. True love is expressed in caring and giving. The word says, for God so Love He gave....

Reach out to someone in need of Jesus. Help someone in crisis find Christ. Look out and prove your love to Jesus by caring and inviting your friends and associates to find Jesus the Healer.

Invite your friends to our Home Care Cell Fellowship (Miracle Chapel Intl. Satellite Fellowship). We're in the U.S. at 33 Schley Street, Newark, New Jersey 07112. Home Care Cell Fellowship Group meets every Tuesday at 6:00pm-7:00pm.

If you are in Nigeria—MIRACLE OF GOD MINISTRIES, aka "MIRACLE CHAPEL INTL." Mpama–Egbu-Owerri Imo state Nigeria.

Chapter 4   Prayer of Salvation

LIFE IS NOT ALL ABOUT DURATION, BUT IT'S ALL ABOUT DONATION

What does this statement mean?

Life consists not in accumulation of material wealth.
Luke 12:15

But it's all about liberality...meaning, what you can give and share with others. *"When you live for others—You live forever"* (Proverbs 11:25) because you outlive your generation by the legacy you live behind after you depart into glory to be with the Lord. But when you live to yourself - you are reduced to self—you are easily forgotten when you die and depart in glory. Permit me to admonish you today to live your life to be a blessing to a soul connected to you today. I want you to know that so many souls are connected and looking up to you, and through you so many souls will be saved and rescued from destruction. Will you disciple someone today to find Jesus Christ?

As a genuine Christian, it is your duty to evangelize Jesus Christ to all you meet on your way. Jesus is still in the healing business-Jesus is still doing miracles from time of old to now. Therefore tell someone about Jesus Christ today, disciple and bring them to Church.

Philip findeth Nathanael...
John 1:45

Please to prove the sincerity of your love for God today; please become a soul winner. The dignity of your Christianity is hidden in your boldness to proclaim and evangelize Jesus Christ to all you meet on your way. There is a question mark on the integrity of your Christianity until you become a life soul winner. Invite someone to join us worship the Lord Jesus this coming Sunday. Amen.

MIRACLE OF GOD MINISTRIES

PILLARS OF THE COMMISSION

We believe, preach and practice the following:

1) We believe and preach Salvation to every living human being.

2) We believe and preach Repentance and Forgiveness of sins.

3) We believe and preach the baptism of the Holy Spirit and Spiritual gifts.

4) We believe and teach Prosperity.

5) We believe and preach Divine Healing and Miracles—Signs and Wonder.

6) We believe and preach Faith.

7) We believe and proclaim the Power of God (Supernatural).

8) We believe and proclaim Praise and Worship to God.

9) We believe and preach Wisdom.

10) We believe and preach Holiness (Consecration).

11) We believe and preach Vision.

12) We believe and teach the Word of God.

13) We believe and teach Success.

14) We believe and practice Prayer.

15) We believe and teach Deliverance.

These 15 stones form the Pillars of Our Commission. Become part of this church family and follow this great move of God.

MY HEARTFELT PRAYER FOR YOU

It is my prayer that you testify today about the goodness of the Lord. I desire for you to have an encounter with our Lord Jesus Christ.

Now let me pray for you:

Heavenly Father, may today be a day of new beginnings for this precious loved one. Lord God of heaven, open a new chapter in the life of this precious loved one reading this book today. May all their secret prayers be answered in the mighty name of Jesus. We thank you Jesus for hearing us. In Jesus' mighty name. Amen.

DO NOT FORGET YOUR GOD

Then beware lest thou forget the Lord, which brought thee forth out of the land of Egypt, from the house of bondage.
Deuteronomy 6:12

In my opinion, knowing God is a personal thing. We are instructed to *"work out your own salvation with fear and trembling. For it is God which worketh in you both to will and to do of his good pleasure."* (Philippians 2:12-13)

It has always been my vision to see you experience an encounter with our Lord Jesus Christ. A lot of church folks have indirectly denied him. But I tell you the truth—as long as you embrace Him invisibly, He will do great things in your life. We must always practice the ritual of daily devotion and prayer as a lifestyle. You can join our prayer line at 515.739.1216 (code 162288) every Monday, Wednesday and Saturday (EST). You can also worship with us at our worship center in New Jersey at 343 Sanford Ave., Newark, NJ 07106.

Do not forget, God is spirit. Therefore we must worship him in spirit and in truth. God is not a man that He should lie, nor the son of man that He should repent. Learn to honor the presence of God in your life. Embrace the acts and hand of God in your life. Respect and revere God in your lifetime. Help spread the gospel of Jesus by winning souls for the Kingdom of God.

Finally, I must talk to you about eternity! Heaven is real and we all must make conscious plans to make it at last. I hate to tell you more about hell, but we must repent of our sins, forsake our sins and confess Jesus as Lord. We must embrace the gift of salvation if we are to enter heaven. We must live a righteous life, worthy of emulation for others to copy, in pursuit of the Kingdom of God.

CHAPTER 5

ABOUT THE AUTHOR

Rev. Franklin N. Abazie is the founding and Presiding Pastor of Miracle of God Ministries, with headquarters in Newark, New Jersey USA and a branch church in Owerri-Imo State Nigeria. He is following the footsteps of one of his mentors, the healing evangelist Oral Roberts of the blessed memory. The Lord passed Oral Roberts' healing mantle two days before he went to be with the Lord at age 91 into the hands of healing evangelist Rev. Franklin N. Abazie in a vision.

In all his services, the Power and Presence of God is present to heal all in his audience. Rev. Abazie is an ordained man of God, with a Healing Ministry reviving the healing and miracle ministry of Jesus Christ of Nazareth.

Pastor Franklin N. Abazie, has been called by God with a unique mandate: **"THE MOMENT IS DUE TO IMPACT YOUR WORLD THROUGH THE REVIVAL OF THE HEALING AND MIRACLE MINISTRY OF JESUS CHRIST OF NAZARETH.**

"I AM SENDING YOU TO RESTORE HEALTH UNTO THEE AND I WILL HEAL THEE OF THY WOUNDS, SAID THE LORD OF HOST."

Chapter 5   About the Author

Rev. Abazie is a gifted, ardent teacher of the word of God, who operates also in the office of a Prophet, generating and attracting undeniable signs and wonders, special miracles and healings, with apostolic fireworks of the Holy Ghost. He is the founding and presiding senior Pastor of this fast growing Healing Ministry. He has written over 86 inspirational, healing and transforming books covering almost all aspects of divine healing and life. He is happily married and blessed with children.

BOOKS BY REV. FRANKLIN N. ABAZIE:

1) *The Outcome of Faith*
2) *Understanding the Secret of Prevailing Prayers*
3) *Commanding Abundance*
4) *Understanding the Secret of the Man God Uses*
5) *Activating My Due Season*
6) *Overcoming Divine Verdicts*
7) *The Outcome of Divine Wisdom*
8) *Understanding God's Restoration Mandate*
9) *Walking In the Victory and Authority of the Truth*
10) *God's Covenant Exemption*
11) *Destiny Restoration Pillars*
12) *Provoking Acceptable Praise*
13) *Understanding Divine Judgment*
14) *Activating Angelic Re-enforcement*
15) *Provoking Un-Merited Favo*
16) *The Benefits of the Speaking Faith*
17) *Understanding Divine Arrangement*
18) *How to Keep Your Healing*
19) *Understanding the Mysteries of the Speaking Faith*
20) *Understanding the Mysteries of Prophetic Healing*
21) *Operating Under the Rules of Creative Healing*
22) *Understanding the Joy of Breakthrough*
23) *Understanding the Mystery of Breakthrough*
24) *Understanding Divine Prosperity*
25) *Understanding Divine Healing*
26) *Retaining Your Inheritance*
27) *Overcoming Confusing Spirit*
28) *Commanding Angelic Escorts*

29) Enforcing Your Inheritance In Christ Jesus
30) Understanding Your Guardian Angels
31) Overcoming the Dominion of Sin
32) Understanding the Voice of God
33) The Outstanding Benefits of the Anointing
34) The Audacity of the Blood of Jesus
35) Walking in the Reality of the Anointing
36) Escaping the Nightmare of Poverty
37) Understanding Your Harvest Season
38) Activating Your Success Buttons
39) Overcoming the Forces of Darkness
40) Overcoming the Devices of the Devil
41) Overcoming Demonic Agents
42) Overcoming the Sorrows of Failure
43) Rejecting the Sorrows of Failure
44) Resisting the Sorrows of Poverty
45) Restoring Broken Marriages
46) Redeeming Your Days
47) The Force of Vision
48) Overcoming the Forces of Ignorance
49) Understanding the Sacrifice of Small Beginning
50) The Might of Small Beginning
51) Understanding the Mysteries of Prophesy
52) Overcoming Dream Nightmares
53) Breaking the Shackles of the Curse of the Law
54) Understanding the Joy of Harvest
55) Wisdom for Signs & Wonders
56) Wisdom for Generational Impact
57) Wisdom for Marriage Stability
58) Understanding the Number of Your Days

59) Enforcing Your Kingdom Rights
60) Escaping the Traps of Immoralities
61) Escaping the Trap of Poverty
62) Accessing Biblical Prosperity
63) Accessing True Riches in Christ
64) Silencing the Voice of the Accuser
65) Overcoming the Forces of Oppositions
66) Quenching the Voice of the Avenger
67) Silencing Demonic Prediction & Projection
68) Silencing Your Mocker
69) Understanding the Power of the Holy Ghost
70) Understanding the Baptism of Power
71) The Mystery of the Blood of Jesus
72) Understanding the Mystery of Sanctification
73) Understanding the Power of Holiness
74) Understanding the Forces of Purity & Righteousness
75) Activating the Forces of Vengeance
76) Appreciating the Mystery of Restoration
77) Overcoming the Projection & Prediction of the Enemy
78) Engaging the Mystery of the Blood
79) Commanding the Power of the Speaking Faith
80) Uprooting the Forces Against Your Rising
81) Overcoming Mere Success Syndrome
82) Understanding Divine Sentence
83) Understanding the Mystery of Praise
84) Understanding the Author of Faith
85) The Mystery of the Finisher of Faith
86) Attracting Supernatural Favor

MIRACLE OF GOD MINISTRIES

NIGERIA CRUSADE 2012

MIRACLE OF GOD MINISTRIES
NIGERIA CRUSADE
2012

MIRACLE OF GOD MINISTRIES
NIGERIA CRUSADE 2012

MIRACLE OF GOD MINISTRIES

NIGERIA CRUSADE

2012

MIRACLE
OF
GOD
MINISTRIES

NIGERIA CRUSADE

2012

www.ingramcontent.com/pod-product-compliance
Lightning Source LLC
Chambersburg PA
CBHW021445080526
44588CB00009B/701